# What's in this book

This book belongs to

T0351539

_____

# 你叫什么名字?
## What is your name?

## 学习内容 Contents

### 沟通 Communication

介绍自己和他人
Introduce yourself and others

询问他人的名字
Ask for someone's name

背景介绍:
刚开学,浩浩和其他小朋友
在校巴站等校巴上学。

### 生词 New words

| | | |
|---|---|---|
| ★ | 你 | you |
| ★ | 我 | I, me |
| ★ | 叫 | to call, to be called |
| ★ | 什么 | what |
| ★ | 名字 | name |
| | 他 | he, him |
| | 她 | she, her |
| | 谢谢 | thanks |

## 句式 Sentence patterns

你叫什么名字？　　　What is your name?

我叫艾文。　　　　　My name is Ivan. (I am called Ivan.)

他叫什么名字？　　　What is his name?

他叫依森。　　　　　His name is Ethan. (He is called Ethan.)

## 文化 Cultures

姓名的排列方式
Order of names

## 跨学科学习 Project

制作图章，介绍自己
Make a name stamp and
introduce yourself

参考答案：
1 They are at the bus stop.
2 They are going to school.
3 Yes, they are queuing behind Hao Hao.

## Get ready

**1** Where are the children?

**2** Where are they going?

**3** Can you find the pair of twins?

故事大意：
浩浩上学不久，认识了一对双胞胎兄弟。
顽皮的弟弟跟浩浩开了个小小的玩笑。

nǐ jiào shén me míng zi
你叫什么名字？

第一次见面，想知道对方的名字时，可以问："你叫什么名字？""你"指的是对方。"什么"一般用在问句里边。提醒学生注意"什么"在句中的位置。

你好！你叫什么名字？

参考问题和答案：

1　Where are the children? (They are at school.)

2　Who is Hao Hao talking to? (He is talking to a blond boy.)

3　Hao Hao wants to know the boy's name. What should he say? ('What's your name?')

❹　4　Do you think Hao Hao knows who this boy is? Why? (No, he does not. Because he is asking for the boy's name.)

伊森的英文名是Ethan。他是哥哥，性格比较老实沉稳。

wǒ jiào ài wén
我叫艾文。

当告诉别人自己的名字时，可以说："我叫……""我"指的是自己。

艾文的英文名是Ivan，他是弟弟，活泼、调皮、好动。

# 我叫艾文，他叫伊森。

参考问题和答案：

1 The blond boy wants to tell Hao Hao his name. What should he say? ('My name is Ivan.')

2 What is on the ground? (A teddy bear.)

3 Does Hao Hao see the teddy bear on the ground? (Yes, he does.)

4 Whose teddy bear do you think it is? Why? (It is Ethan's teddy bear. Because his school bag is open.)

# 伊森，这是你的玩具熊。

参考问题和答案：

1. What did Hao Hao do with the teddy bear on the ground? (He picked it up and took it with him to the classroom.)
2. What does Hao Hao want to do with the teddy bear now? (He wants to give it back to Ethan.)
3. Which of the twin brothers is Hao Hao talking to? (He is talking to Ivan.)

# 浩浩，谢谢！

当别人帮助了自己，可以说："谢谢！"

参考问题和答案：

1 Does Hao Hao know that he gave the teddy bear to Ivan, not Ethan? (No, he does not.)
2 Ivan accepts the teddy bear from Hao Hao. What is he saying to Hao Hao? ('Thank you!')
3 What is Ethan searching his school bag for? (He is searching for the teddy bear.)

# 你叫什么名字？

参考问题和答案：

1 Is the blond boy Ivan or Ethan? How do you know? (He is Ethan. He has fewer freckles on his face.)

2 What is Ethan doing? (He is asking Hao Hao about his teddy bear.)

3 Why is Hao Hao asking for Ethan's name? (Because Hao Hao is wondering why Ethan is asking about the teddy bear again. He thinks he already gave it back. And since Ethan and Ivan look the same, he does not know who he is talking to.)

我叫伊森，他叫艾文。

参考问题和答案：

1　How does Hao Hao look? (He looks confused.)
2　Why do you think Ivan took Ethan's teddy bear from Hao Hao? (Because he wants to play
　　a trick on Hao Hao.)

# Let's think

**1** Number the pictures. Act out the story.

**2** Circle the differences between the twins and say their names.

伊森　　　　艾文

# New words

**1** Learn the new words.

**2** Match the words to the pictures. Write the letters.

a 你　　　b 我　　　c 名字　　　d 什么

1 b　　2 d　　3 c　　4 a

# 听听说说 Listen and say

 **1** Look, listen and repeat.

 **2** Look at the pictures. Listen to the st

**1**

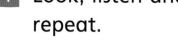

**2**

**3**

**4**

你叫什么名字？

他叫什么名字？

nd say.

**3** Tick and say the correct sentence.

什么名字你叫？

✓ 你叫什么名字？

**4** Talk with your friend.

# Task

提醒学生用中文"你叫什么名字？"来问朋友的名字，待朋友说"我叫……"后才写下朋友的名字。可以写朋友的英文名。

Find out the names of your friends.
Write them on the name tags.

你叫什么名字？

# Game

Listen to your teacher. Point to the words and work out the sentences.

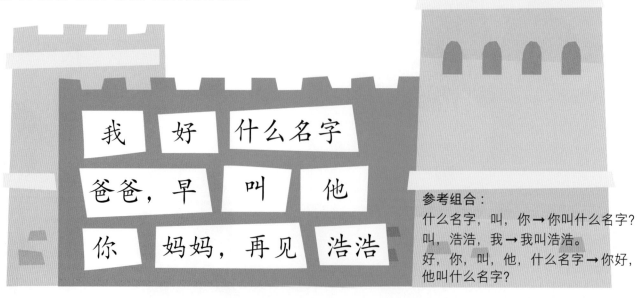

我　好　什么名字

爸爸，早　叫　他

你　妈妈，再见　浩浩

参考组合：
什么名字，叫，你 → 你叫什么名字？
叫，浩浩，我 → 我叫浩浩。
好，你，叫，他，什么名字 → 你好，他叫什么名字？

# Song

🎧 **Listen and sing.**

你好！你好！

你好吗？

你叫什么名字？

我很好呀，我很好！

我叫浩浩！

你叫什么名字？

我叫浩浩。

延伸活动：
学生大合唱，每次唱到最后一句时，老师随机指向一位学生，该学生需将该句歌词中的"浩浩"换成自己的名字再唱出。

## 课堂用语 Classroom language

很好。
Very good.

对。
Correct.

不对。
Incorrect.

对不对？
Is it correct?

# 写一写 Write

**1** **Learn and trace the stroke.** 老师示范笔画动作，学生跟着做：用手在空中画出"撇"。

撇

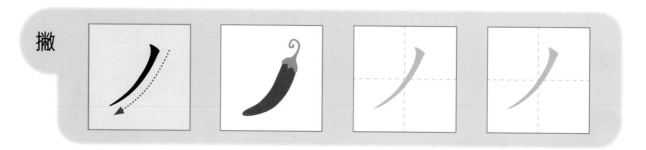

**2** **Learn the component. Trace 亻 to complete the characters.**

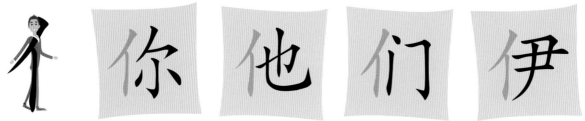

学生观察图片，引导他们发现单人旁与人有关。

**3** **How many 亻 can you find in the picture? Circle them.**
视情况提醒学生树上、花丛中以及男孩和女孩的身上都有该部件。

**4** **Trace and write the character.** 提醒学生"你"字的书写顺序为从左到右。可结合"汉字小常识"告诉他们左右结构的汉字的书写顺序都是从左到右。

ノ　イ　イ　䦹　你　你　你

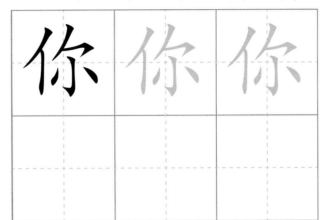

**5** **Write and say.**

你　叫什么名字？

汉字 小常识 *Did you know?*

Some characters are made up of left and right components.

**Colour the left component red and the right component green.**

红色　绿色

红色　绿色

红色　绿色

红色　绿色

该结构中的左右部件所占比例不一定相同。上方的字有的是左窄右宽，
如"你""好""什"和"他"；"叫"字则是左右等宽。

**17**

# 多元学习 Connections

## Cultures

中国人的姓以单字最为常见，如：李、王、张、刘、陈等。也有一些由两个字或以上的汉字组成的复姓，如：欧阳、司马等。而名则通常由一至两个字组成。

**1** **What is the difference between Chinese and Western names?**

Chinese names start with the family name.

王 小 玲　丁 浩

Elsa　Lopez

Western names usually end with the family name.

Peter　George　Dixon

延伸活动：
老师根据学生的本名帮他们起中文名，然后学生用中文询问其他同学的中文名。

**2** **Colour the family names red and the first names blue.**

这是中间名 (middle name)，中文姓名没有中间名。

红色　　蓝色　　　蓝色　　　　　　　　红色

丁　玲　Ethan　Joseph　Jones

# Project

材料：一支铅笔、一块橡皮、
一张便利贴、一管红色颜料。

## 1 Make yourself a name stamp.

② 用铅笔在便利贴上
写下自己的名字。

③ 将便利贴有名字的一面
反过来紧贴橡皮。

Alice

用铅笔尾部反复摩
擦有名字的部分。

Be careful!

⑤ 用铅笔尖将橡皮上的
名字挖空。

⑥ 将橡皮印章带有名字的
一面在红色颜料里沾上
颜料，就可以使用啦！

## 2 Stamp your name below and say it.

我叫 Alice。你叫
什么名字？

Alice

# 温习 Checkpoint

游戏方法:

学生从"Start"开始,依次正确回答小径上面设置的七道题才能在终点帮伊森找回玩具熊。提醒学生第4题使用完整中句式表述,但名字可以用英文;第6题也需使用完整中文句一边指着对应人物,一边说出其姓名。

**1** Ethan lost his teddy bear. Help him find it.

Finish

Write 'you' in Chinese.

你

**2** Work with your friend. Colour the stars and the chillies.

| Words and sentences | 说 | 读 | 写 |
|---|---|---|---|
| 你 | ☆ | ☆ | ☆ |
| 我 | ☆ | ☆ | 🌶 |
| 叫 | ☆ | ☆ | 🌶 |
| 什么 | ☆ | ☆ | 🌶 |
| 名字 | ☆ | ☆ | 🌶 |
| 他 | ☆ | 🌶 | 🌶 |
| 她 | ☆ | 🌶 | 🌶 |
| 谢谢 | ☆ | 🌶 | 🌶 |
| 你叫什么名字？ | ☆ | 🌶 | 🌶 |
| 我叫浩浩。 | ☆ | 🌶 | 🌶 |

| | |
|---|---|
| Introduce yourself and others | ☆ |
| Ask for someone's name | ☆ |

评核建议：

根据学生课堂表现，分别给予"太棒了！(Excellent!)"、"不错！(Good!)"或"继续努力！(Work harder!)"的评价，再让学生圈出左侧对应的表情，以记录自己的学习情况。

**3** What does your teacher say?

My teacher says ...

21

# 分享 Sharing

## Words I remember

| | | |
|---|---|---|
| 你 | nǐ | you |
| 我 | wǒ | I, me |
| 叫 | jiào | to call, to be called |
| 什么 | shén me | what |
| 名字 | míng zi | name |
| 他 | tā | he, him |
| 她 | tā | she, her |
| 谢谢 | xiè xie | thanks |

# Other words

| | | |
|---|---|---|
| 伊森 | yī sēn | Ethan |
| 艾文 | ài wén | Ivan |
| 这 | zhè | this |
| 是 | shì | to be |
| 的 | de | of |
| 玩具熊 | wán jù xióng | teddy bear |

延伸活动：
1 学生用手遮盖英文，读中文单词，并思考单词意思；
2 学生用手遮盖中文单词，看着英文说出对应的中文单词；
3 学生三人一组，尽量运用中文单词分角色复述故事。

# OXFORD

**UNIVERSITY PRESS**

Oxford University Press is a department of the University of Oxford.
It furthers the University's objective of excellence in research, scholarship,
and education by publishing worldwide. Oxford is a registered trade mark of
Oxford University Press in the UK and in certain other countries

Published in Hong Kong by
Oxford University Press (China) Limited
39th Floor, One Kowloon, 1 Wang Yuen Street, Kowloon Bay,
Hong Kong

Illustrated by Anne Lee and Wildman

Photographs for reproduction permitted by Dreamstime.com

China National Publications Import & Export (Group) Corporation is an authorized distributor of
Oxford Elementary Chinese.

Please contact content@cnpiec.com.cn or 86-10-65856782

ISBN: 978-0-19-942969-1

10 9 8 7 6 5 4 3 2


Teacher's Edition
ISBN: 978-0-19-082148-7

10 9 8 7 6 5 4 3 2